LEGENDS OF WARFARE

AVIATION

B-17 Flying Fortress, Vol. 2

Boeing's B-17E through B-17H in World War II

DAVID DOYLE

SCHIFFER MILITARY

4880 Lower Valley Road   Atglen, PA 19310

Front cover photo courtesy of Rick Kolasa
Designed by Justin Watkinson
Type set in Impact/Minion Pro/Univers LT Std

ISBN: 978-0-7643-6129-6
Printed in China

Published by Schiffer Publishing, Ltd.
4880 Lower Valley Road
Atglen, PA 19310
Phone: (610) 593-1777; Fax: (610) 593-2002
E-mail: Info@schifferbooks.com
www.schifferbooks.com

For our complete selection of fine books on this and related subjects, please visit our website at www.schifferbooks.com. You may also write for a free catalog.

Schiffer Publishing's titles are available at special discounts for bulk purchases for sales promotions or premiums. Special editions, including personalized covers, corporate imprints, and excerpts, can be created in large quantities for special needs. For more information, contact the publisher.

We are always looking for people to write books on new and related subjects. If you have an idea for a book, please contact us at proposals@schifferbooks.com.

Acknowledgments

I have been blessed with the generous help of many friends and colleagues when preparing this manuscript. Truly, this book would not have been possible without their collective assistance. Tom Kailbourn, Stan Piet, Scott Taylor, Dana Bell, Rich Kolasa, Bill Larkins, the staff at the San Diego Air and Space Museum, the staff at the Air Force Historical Research Agency, and Brett Stolle at the National Museum of the United States Air Force all gave of their time without hesitation. My lovely and dear wife, Denise, scanned photos, proofread manuscripts, and was my personal cheerleader throughout the difficult parts of this project, and without her unflagging support this could not have been completed.

All photos are from the collection of the National Museum of the United States Air Force, unless otherwise noted.

Contents

Introduction   004

CHAPTER 1   **B-17E**   006

CHAPTER 2   **XB-38**   034

CHAPTER 3   **B-17F**   044

CHAPTER 4   **X/YB-40**   080

CHAPTER 5   **B-17G**   086

CHAPTER 6   **B-17H/SB-17G**   124

Introduction

When the gleaming Model 299, the experimental prototype of what would become the B-17, was unveiled on July 17, 1935, *Seattle Times* reporter Richard L. Williams wrote, "Declared to be the largest land plane ever built in America, this fifteen-ton flying fortress, built by the Boeing Aircraft Co.," thereby giving the aircraft its name, which endures to this day.

Representing a significant advance in aircraft design compared to other US bombers of the era, those early B-17s were invaluable in proving the concept of high-altitude, long-range strategic bombing. However, the early B-17s were far from flying fortresses, as combat experience in Europe and the Pacific would quickly prove. The aircraft lacked armor, some of them lacked self-sealing fuel tanks, and all were woefully underarmed. When introduced, the B-17 could fly higher and as fast or faster than most of its adversaries; however, by the time war actually broke out in Europe, both of those advantages had been overtaken. The B-17s would be met head on, both figuratively and literally, at altitude, and an improved model was needed.

Specifications			
	B-17E	**B-17F**	**B-17G**
Armament:	1 × .30 cal. + 8 × .50 cal.	11 × .50 cal.	12 × .50 cal.
Bombload:	4,200 lbs.	8,000 lbs.	8,000 lbs.
Engines (4 ×):	Wright R-1820-65, 1,200 hp	Wright R-1820-97, 1,200 hp	Wright R-1820-97, 1,200 hp
Max. speed:	317 mph @ 25,000 ft.	325 mph @ 25,000 ft.	302 mph @ 25,000 ft.
Cruise speed:	226 mph	160 mph	160 mph
Service ceiling:	36,000 ft.	37,500 ft.	35,600 ft.
Range:	3,200 miles	4,220 miles	3,400 miles
Wingspan:	103 ft., 9 in.	103 ft., 9 in.	103 ft., 9 in.
Length:	73 ft., 10 in.	74 ft., 9 in.	74 ft., 9 in.
Height:	19 ft., 2 in.	19 ft., 1 in.	19 ft., 1 in.
Weight (gross):	51,000 lbs.	56,500 lbs.	65,500 lbs.
Number built:	512	3,405	8,680
Serial numbers:	41-2393 to 41-2669, 41-9011 to 41-9245	Boeing: 41-24340 to 24639, 42-5050 to 42-5484, 42-29467 to 42-31031; Douglas: 42-2964 to 42-3562, 42-37714 to 42-27720; Vega: 42-5705 to 42-6204	Boeing: 42-31032 to 42-32116, 42-97058 to 42-97407, 42-102379 to 42-102978, 43-37509 to 43-39508; Douglas: 42-37716, 42-37721 to 42-38213, 42-106984 to 42-107233, 44-6001 to 44-7000, 44-83236 to 44-83885; Vega: 42-39758 to 42-40057, 42-97436 to 42-98035, 44-8001 to 44-9000, 44-85492 to 44-85841

The Y1B-17 was the service-test version of the Flying Fortress and precursor to an illustrious and ever-evolving line of strategic bombers. As seen in a photo of Y1B-17, serial number 36-161, flying above the Brooklyn, New York, docks around the late 1930s, the initial design of the plane included such elements as a tapering rear fuselage without a tail turret, a dorsal fin with a leading edge that joined the top of the fuselage abruptly, propeller spinners, and blister-type machine gun turrets.

The B-17B was the first production model of the Flying Fortress. The first example, serial number 38-211, is seen here with markings for the Army Air Corps' Materiel Division at Wright Field, Ohio. By now, the blister turrets on the nose and above the radio operator's compartment had been eliminated, the latter being replaced by clear panels that, with revisions, would remain a feature of subsequent B-17 models. The waist blisters had been replaced by flatter, teardrop-shaped windows.

CHAPTER 1
B-17E

By early 1940, it was clear that the B-17 would not be able to operate out of reach of enemy aircraft, and thus a dramatic increase in armament would be required. Boeing engineers essentially redesigned the fuselage from the cockpit back. While the increase of armament brought about through this redesign is obvious, less obvious were sweeping internal changes as well. In total, over 400 changes were made to the B-17 design with the introduction of the new type. Given the Boeing designation Model 299-O, the model number that would be retained to the end of B-17 production, the improved bomber was designated the B-17E by the Army Air Force.

The redesigned and enlarged fuselage added a tail gunner's position, armed with twin .50-caliber machine guns, beneath and behind a massive new vertical stabilizer. The new stabilizer replaced the shark fin tail used on the earlier models, and completely altered the profile of the B-17.

Atop the fuselage, just aft of the pilots' seats, was a power-operated Sperry A-1 top turret sporting twin .50-caliber machine guns. Manned by the B-17's flight engineer, the top turret was a vital defensive position. Not only could the guns be brought to bear along the sides of the B-17, they were also tasked with defending the aircraft from overhead or frontal attacks.

On either side of the fuselage were improved waist gun positions with large, open windows, which, while permitting a wide field of vision and fire, also opened the aircraft to enormous blasts of air, which at the altitudes the bombers flew at was well below freezing, often in the −50-degree Fahrenheit range. Such temperatures meant that the B-17 gunners wore insulated and electrically heated flight suits—and were often still cold.

Beneath the bomber, rather than the bathtub gun position used on the B-17D, was a Sperry number 645705-D turret. This streamlined turret, armed with a pair of .50-caliber machine guns, is often mistaken for a similar Bendix turret. The turret is operated by remote control, with the gunner lying prone on the floor and sighting through a periscope arrangement.

All of these improvements brought with them an increase in the bomber's length, adding 6 feet, and weight, with the top turret alone adding 700 pounds. In total, 2,500 pounds was added to the aircraft, yet, remarkably, owing to the careful and deliberate work of Boeing engineers, the top speed of the B-17E was only 6 miles per hour less then the B-17D, despite using the same R-1820-65 engines. Even more surprising, cruising speed dropped a mere 1 mile per hour.

The Army Air Force ordered 150 of the B-17E on June 17, 1940, thirteen months before the first B-17 saw combat. A further 127 of the type were added to the order on July 12, meaning that at last, the B-17 was going into mass production. On September 16, an additional 235 B-17s were placed on order.

The first B-17E took to the air on September 5, 1941. When reports from Europe reached the Army Air Force detailing the problems that the RAF was having with their Fortress Is (modified B-17Cs), which entered combat on July 8, 1941—specifically, only two hits in thirty-nine bombing missions, at a cost of eight lost aircraft—the US Army knew that major changes were justified.

The remote-control Sperry 645705-D belly turret was never popular, being awkward to use and sometimes unreliable. Thus, from the 113th onward, a different belly turret was used, which was the famous Sperry A-2 ball turret. With this, the gunner was inside the turret itself, in a fetal position, with a machine gun to either side. Entry to the turret could be made either from on the ground or in the aircraft, as dictated by the turret position. While the gunner could bail out directly from the turret if need be, many ball turret gunners left their parachutes in the fuselage in order to provide a little more space in the cramped turret. As a result, in the event of an emergency the gunner had to position the turret in the proper manner to exit into the aircraft, don his parachute, then bail out. Statistically speaking, most wounds to ball turret gunners were fatal, but the ball turret gunner was least likely of any of the B-17 gunners to be hit at all: the tail gunner's position was the most dangerous of the gunners' positions.

While in the Pacific the B-17E as well as earlier models of Flying Fortresses were subjected to the Japanese attacks of December 7 and 8, in Europe it was the B-17E that the US servicemen first flew into combat.

The B-17E was a major step forward from the preceding models of the Flying Fortress, seeing the addition of powered Sperry top and bottom machine-gun turrets, new waist windows, enlarged aft fuselage with a tail turret, and other improvements. It was the first B-17 model to be built in the hundreds, with 517 being completed. Of particular notice, as seen in this photo of the first B-17E, serial number 41-2393, is the elimination of the former vertical tail with its "shark" fin, in favor of a much-enlarged fin and rudder.

The fuselage of the B-17E from the cockpit to the nose remained similar to that of the B-17D. The engines were the Wright R-1820-65 Cyclones. An important change on the B-17E was the deletion of the "bathtub" machine gun gondola on the belly aft of the bomb bay, replaced by a Sperry number 645705-D remote-controlled turret (sometimes mistakenly referred to as a Bendix turret) on the belly, in conjunction with a Plexiglas dome for a gunsight aft of the turret. Also, a Sperry A-1 dorsal turret was installed just aft of the cockpit canopy.

The engines of the first B-17E, serial number 41-2393, are being checked at the Boeing factory. The first flight for this plane was on September 5, 1941. The B-17Es retained the flexible socket mounts for machine guns on the front end: two on the clear nose, one on the overhead window, and one each on the center left cheek window and the front right cheek window.

The same engine-testing session for the first B-17E is viewed from a lower and closer perspective. A visible change from the preceding models of the B-17 was the addition of an oil-cooler air intake for each engine, with two intakes mounted on the leading edge of each wing between the two engines. A deicer boot is between the two oil-cooler intakes on the left wing. The other intakes on the leading edges of the wings, arranged in pairs, were for supercharger ram air and intercooler air.

The Sperry A-1 dorsal turret on this B-17E is a dark color, probably Olive Drab, contrasting with the unpainted aluminum finish of the bomber. The right-side entry door on the aft part of the fuselage had been moved aft of the waist window and now was of a rectangular shape, with a square window. The horizontal tailplanes on the B-17E were enlarged, to provide better stability during bombing runs.

The relative positions of the Sperry number 645705-D remote-controlled ventral turret and the smaller, Plexiglas sighting dome for the turret are visible on the belly of the fuselage aft of the wings. On each side of the fuselage, above the sighting dome, were two short, wide windows for the gunner.
Air Force Historical Research Agency

A Sperry number 645705-D ventral turret is viewed facing aft, with the sighting dome behind it. The Browning .50-caliber machine gun barrels have the early-type cooling sleeves with elongated cooling slots. The light-colored object to the upper right is the fairlead (a guide tube) and weight for a trailing antenna, a wire antenna with a weight attached to the rear end of it, which would be paid out to the rear of the aircraft. *National Archives*

The fuselage interior of a B-17E is viewed facing aft. In the lower foreground is the bottom gunner's sight, which involved a complicated system of mirrors and a gunsight on a turntable. Just aft of the bottom gunner's station are the waist windows; the waist machine-gun mounts are not present. The drum-shaped object in the background is a chemical toilet, to the rear of which is the wheel well for the tail landing gear. Opposite to and slightly forward of the chemical toilet are two engine-servicing platforms in their stored positions. These would be attached to the engine nacelles to provide platforms for mechanics while working on the engines. *National Archives*

Below the bottom gunner's sight was a Plexiglas dome, through which the bottom of the sighting system is visible. The sight moved in sync with the movements of the bottom turret. Above the dome are a small port with a door, apparently to allow the gunner to wipe off the Plexiglas dome if necessary, and two rectangular windows for the gunner. *National Archives*

The bottom gunner's sighting station is viewed facing forward, showing the gunsight, mounted on a yoke, and the gunner's kneeling pad, which is lying on a pan of thin armor plate. To the front, part of the ring for the bottom turret is visible. The Sperry bottom turret arrangement was a poor one: for example, the arrangements for the sight and the gunner's accommodations were very awkward, often resulting in problems such as vertigo for the gunner while he was operating the turret. *National Archives*

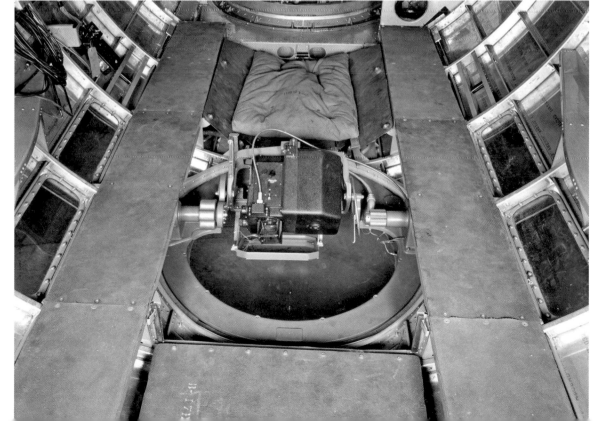

A B-17E in Olive Drab over Neutral Gray camouflage cruises above a shoreline, probably in Washington State or the Pacific Northwest. The national insignia is the type with the red circle in the center, used up to early May 1942. The domes on the Hamilton Standard Hydromatic propeller hubs, which housed the hydraulic pitch-changing piston, were painted matte black. *Air Force Historical Research Agency*

The first B-17E, serial number 41-2393, started out with a natural-aluminum finish, but by the time this photo was taken it was painted in matte Olive Drab over Neutral Gray. Under the nose is a radio direction finder "football" antenna. *National Museum of Naval Aviation*

The B-17E had a retractable tail landing gear, but no doors were fitted to the gear bay. The open bay is visible on the bottom of the fuselage aft of the entry door.

A mix of Navy and Army Air Forces aircraft were dispatched to Naval Air Station Midway, on East Midway Island, in advance of the June 1942 Battle of Midway. This B-17E from the 72nd Bombardment Squadron, 5th Bombardment Group, is parked alongside a sandbag revetment on East Midway Island around the time of the battle. Color motion-picture footage of this plane shows that its upper surfaces were coated in at least three different shades of camouflage paint. Note the .30-caliber machine gun barrel in the socket on the center cheek window.

An original color photograph depicts a B-17E parked on grass at an unidentified location. The main landing-gear oleo struts are painted in what appears to be light gray, and seems to be of a lighter tone than the Neutral Gray paint on the lower part of the aircraft. *National Archives*

The Sperry remote-controlled lower turret never proved to be an effective weapon, but starting with B-17E, serial number 41-2504, a very effective, new turret was installed in the belly in the form of the Sperry ball turret. In this turret, the gunner and the twin Browning .50-caliber machine guns moved together, through azimuth and elevation, making for much-easier acquisition and tracking of fast-moving targets. A Sperry ball turret installation is in this B-17E, serial number 41-2567, shown with bomb-bay doors open. *Air Force Historical Research Agency*

A late-production B-17E, serial number 41-9196, is viewed from above, showing the markings on the wings. The occasion was ceremonial: a VIP stand with seats is to the front of the plane. While assigned to the 30th Bombardment Squadron, 19th Bombardment Group, 5th Air Force, this Flying Fortress failed to return from a bombing mission to Rabaul on October 5, 1942, and the crew was declared missing in action.

The cockpit of a B-17E is depicted in a photograph dated September 18, 1941, showing the seats, control columns, pedestal, rudder pedals, and main instrument panel. The curved yokes of the control columns continued to be made of laminated wood.

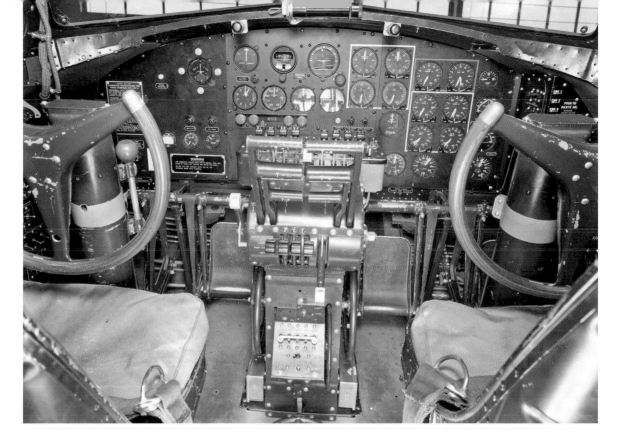

The pedestal between the pilot's and copilot's seats is shown close-up. The throttle controls (*bottom*) were shaped like inverted Ls and could be moved separately or all together at once. To the front of the left throttle controls are four turbosupercharger controls, marked B1 through B4, to the right of which are the four fuel-mixture control levers

To the left is the right side of the main instrument panel. To the right is a panel with engine-oil dilution controls, engine starter switches, and fire extinguisher controls.

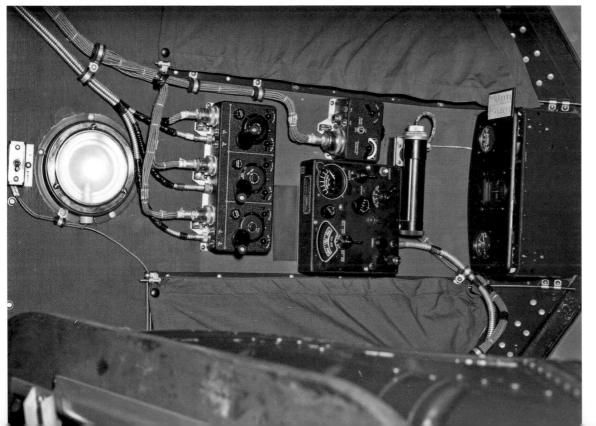

The instruments and controls on the ceiling of the cockpit are shown, with the top of the windscreen to the far right. To the left is a dome light, to the front of which are radio controls, by which the pilot and copilot could operate, to some extent, the plane's radio systems except for the liaison set. To the right is a panel with a clock, compass, and free-air thermometer.

In a photo of part of the left wall of a B-17E taken on May 30, 1942, at the top is the pilot's oxygen regulator, below which is a panel with various switches and gauges, including ammeters, generator switches, and a voltmeter. Below this panel is the pilot's bomb-release handle. Note the "Flying Fortress" logo plate and the oval serial number (not legible) plate on the instrument panel to the upper right. Slightly forward of these, on the top of the pedestal, are ignition switches (*far left*), fuel-boost pump switches, fuel-shutoff-valve switches, cowl-flap controls, and switches for the landing gear and wing flaps.

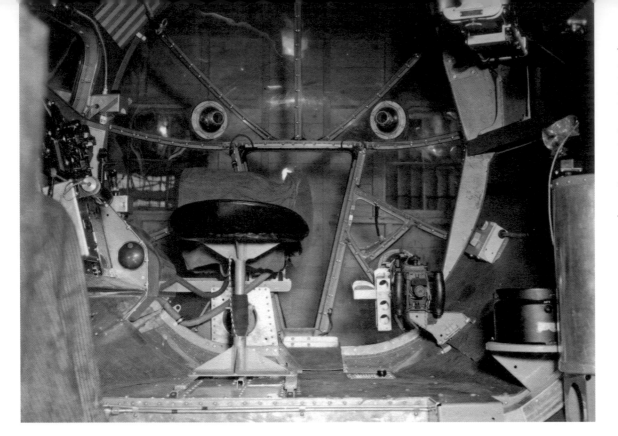

The bombardier's compartment is viewed from the rear in a photo taken May 9, 1942. To the left of center is the bombardier's seat, to the front of which is the Norden bombsight under a cover. On the top half of the clear nose are two flexible sockets for installing a machine gun. The barrel of a fixed machine gun protrudes through the lower-right part of the clear nose. To the upper right is a .30-caliber machine gun mounted in the socket in the forward right cheek window.

The bombardier was provided with a control panel on the left wall of his compartment. At the upper left are gauges, including air speed indicator, altimeter, clock, and free-air thermometer. To the upper right are light and communications switches and bomb-indicator control knob. On the bottom are, *center*, the intervalometer, which controlled the time sequence of bomb releases, and, *right*, the bomb indicator.

The same bombardier's control panel is viewed from the rear. The dark, tube-shaped object on the lower left of the panel is an ultraviolet spotlight.

On the wedge-shaped bracket mounted on the front of the bombardier's control panel (*left*) is a small box containing the bomb-release switch. Below the bomb-release switch are the control levers for the bomb-bay door and the bomb-release mechanism. To the right is the cover over the Norden bombsight.

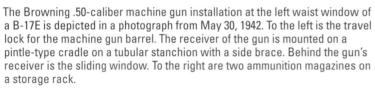

The Browning .50-caliber machine gun installation at the left waist window of a B-17E is depicted in a photograph from May 30, 1942. To the left is the travel lock for the machine gun barrel. The receiver of the gun is mounted on a pintle-type cradle on a tubular stanchion with a side brace. Behind the gun's receiver is the sliding window. To the right are two ammunition magazines on a storage rack.

The right-hand waist machine-gun installation in a B-17E is viewed in the stowed position, facing aft, in a photograph taken May 30, 1942. On the interior of the fuselage skin are factory-stenciled markings, including "ALC24S-T," which indicates Alcoa Alclad, which was corrosion-resistant sheet aluminum formed from high-strength aluminum alloy sandwiched between surface layers of high-purity aluminum.

Boeing B-17E, serial number 41-9131, is viewed from below in flight with "U.S. ARMY" markings on the wings and prewar national insignia on the right wing and the aft fuselage.

B-17E fuselage assemblies are on the Boeing assembly line in 1941 or 1942. Originally, a manufacturing pool of Boeing, Douglas Aircraft, and the Vega Division of Lockheed was to have shared in the assembly of B-17Es, but delays in implementing the plan resulted in the B-17F being the first model of Flying Fortress to be built by the manufacturing pool.

Two rows of aft fuselage sections are under construction at the Boeing plant in Seattle around early January 1942. In the foreground, the forward part of the dorsal fin has been installed on a fuselage section. The turret sections at the rear of the fuselages remain to be installed, as well as the rudders and the remainder of the dorsal fins.

The interior of an aft fuselage section is viewed from just aft of the waist windows, facing to the rear. In the background is bulkhead 7, which had a large opening in it and two vertical braces.

Nicknamed "Tugboat Annie" early on, B-17E, serial number 41-2599, was paid for by donations from citizens of Portland, Oregon. This photo evidently shows the aircraft flying over the Pacific Northwest before its deployment to the Southwest Pacific, where it served with the 19th and 43rd Bombardment Groups. The bomber was lost after an emergency landing on water off New Guinea on January 16, 1943.

The next aircraft in construction sequence after the one nicknamed "Tugboat Annie" was nicknamed "Esmeralda" (B-17E, serial number 41-2600). Its nickname is painted in yellow script below the right cheek windows. *Air Force Historical Research Agency*

"Esmeralda" is seen in another vintage color photo. The national insignia is the type authorized from May 1942 to June 1943. The plane exhibits noticeable weathering and oil staining. *Air Force Historical Research Agency*

Boeing B-17Es, serial numbers 41-9141 and 41-9131, fly above a cloud layer over the United States. The closer aircraft, 41-9141, is painted in RAF daylight-bombing camouflage colors (Dark Earth and Dark Green over Azure Blue) and has a red, white, and blue flash on the dorsal fin, while the other plane appears to be painted in US Army Air Forces camouflage of Olive Drab over Neutral Gray. Apparently, 41-9141 was originally intended for transfer to the British, but neither plane in this photo ever served outside the United States. *Air Force Historical Research Agency*

Paul Tibbets, who gained fame at the end of World War II by commanding the B-29 nicknamed "Enola Gay" in the atomic strike against Hiroshima, Japan, flew his first combat mission in this B-17E, serial number 41-2578. At the time the aircraft was nicknamed "Butcher Shop" and was assigned to the 340th Bombardment Squadron, 97th Bombardment Group, at Polebrook, England. The plane also served with several other squadrons during the war. *Roger Freeman*

An armorer is passing inert practice bombs from a bomb trailer to the bomb bay of a B-17E. Note the red caution flag on the front of the trailer bed. *Air Force Historical Research Agency*

Three men in the waist compartment of a B-17E are enjoying a meal of bottled milk and sandwiches. In the background is bulkhead number 6, with the open door leading into the radio compartment. Although difficult to see, on this side of the door is a black, pyramidal-shaped cover for the support structure of the ball turret. *Air Force Historical Research Agency*

A B-17E that suffered a landing-gear collapse has been lifted by inflatable rubber bags during recovery efforts at the 11th Combat Crew Replacement Center, Army Air Forces Station No. 112 (RAF Bovingdon), England, on December 5, 1944. These bags were employed in recovery efforts when there was a danger of damaging the aluminum skin by using other methods, such as jacks. *National Archives*

While taxiing in a powerful crosswind at Fort Glenn, Alaska, on December 4, 1942, the right brake of this B-17E, serial number 41-9205, failed, resulting in the plane crashing into an embankment. The plane was repaired and returned to service, but tragedy struck ten months later, when five crewmen died after the plane made a forced landing on Lake Bennett, Yukon Territory.

"Typhoon McGoon II," B-17E, serial number 41-9211, was equipped with ASV radar antennas on the nose and under the wings while serving with the 98th Bombardment Squadron, 11th Bombardment Group, on New Caledonia in early 1943. A scoreboard of six Japanese flags and six bomb symbols is below the nickname. *National Archives*

A Boeing B-17E nicknamed "Big Stoop" is seen after crash-landing in Greenland in July 1942. This plane had been modified with enlarged cheek windows with mounts for .50-caliber machine guns, at the center-window position on the left side, as seen here, and on the front position on the right side.

A B-17E numbered 95 and nicknamed "Rhett Butler" is warming its engines, while a B-17F stands by in the background. The contrast in the designs of the clear noses of the two models of Flying Fortress is evident. The plane's serial number on the nomenclature and data stencil below the aft cheek window is not entirely legible, but the number was in the 41-2500 range. *Air Force Historical Research Agency*

CHAPTER 2
XB-38

As a hedge against possible future shortages of Wright Cyclone engines, in July 1942 the Army Air Forces tasked the Vega Division of Lockheed, part of the manufacturing pool for the Flying Fortresses, with experimenting with mounting Allison V-1710-89 V-12 liquid-cooled engines on the airframe of B-17E, serial number 41-2401. Vega designated the plane the Model V-134-1, and the USAAF designation was XB-38. As seen here, new engine nacelles and spinners were installed. A mock ball turret is on the belly.

As we will see in the next chapter, demand for the B-17 soon outstripped Boeing's production capability. One of the firms contracted to augment Boeing's production was Vega Aircraft Corporation, a subsidiary of Lockheed. In hopes both of improving performance of the B-17 as well as providing an alternative power plant in the event demand outstripped production of the Wright R-1820, Vega proposed installing the Allison V-1710-89 liquid-cooled V-12 engine. Lockheed-Vega was well acquainted with the Allison, since it was the power plant of the P-38 Lightning.

Vega assigned their proposal the model number V-134-1 and projected that with four 1,425-horsepower Allisons replacing four 1,200-horsepower Wrights, in addition to the more streamlined engine installation, the new aircraft would readily exceed the performance of the standard B-17. While initially Vega had proposed to build the new aircraft from the ground up, on July 10, 1942, a contract was signed that provided that the XB-38 would be converted from an existing airframe.

Boeing B-17E, serial number 41-2401, the ninth B-17E built, had previously been supplied to Vega as a sample prior to the company initiating production of Flying Fortresses. With Vega B-17 production underway, 41-2401 was no longer needed as a sample and was made available for the conversion. The military designation of the V-134-1 was the XB-38.

Vega technicians removed the wings and began the myriad of modifications needed for the installation of the liquid-cooled engines, including the installation of radiators and oil coolers, along with the related plumbing. Naturally the motor mounts had

to be changed as well. As Studebaker began producing the R-1820 under license, in vast quantities, the concern of an inadequate supply and thus the need for an alternative power plant was abated. Ultimately, Studebaker produced 63,789 R-1820-65 and R-1820-97 engines, over half of all R-1820s built.

With the pressure relieved some, work on the XB-38 project slowed somewhat, and it was May 1943 before the aircraft was ready for flight testing. The maiden flight was May 19, 1943, with Lockheed's Bud Martin as pilot and George MacDonald as copilot.

After the sixth test flight the XB-38 was grounded when leaks were discovered in the exhaust manifold joints, which had the potential to cause a fire. After repairs, the test program resumed.

On June 16, 1943, with Martin and MacDonald again at the controls, the XB-38 lifted into the air for its ninth test flight. However, during the flight a fire broke out in the number 3 engine nacelle. Martin activated the onboard fire extinguishers for that engine, which temporarily lessened but did not extinguish the flames, which continued to creep across the wing toward the main fuel tank. Navigating toward an uninhabited area, Martin set the autopilot and he and MacDonald and four other crewman bailed out. Unfortunately, both pilots' parachutes failed to operate properly. MacDonald's chute failed to open, and he was killed. Martin's parachute did not completely open, and he was severely injured—although he ultimately recovered and resumed flying. The unmanned XB-38, its burning number 3 engine having fallen off, crashed into the floor of California's Central Valley, near Tipton, and burned.

Subsequently, the XB-38 project was abandoned.

The one-off XB-38 is parked on a tarmac. The overall finish was aluminum. Black deicer boots were on the fronts of the wings, the dorsal fin, and the horizontal stabilizers. On the chins of the cowlings were air scoops for the oil coolers.

On the leading edge of each wing between the engine nacelles on the XB-38 were air inlets for the radiators, which were enclosed in the wings and served to cool the Allison V-1710-89 liquid-cooled engines.

The XB-38 had retained the Plexiglas sighting dome and the two rectangular windows for the bottom gunner on each side of the fuselage, which were present on the early B-17Es before the introduction of the Sperry ball turret. For the XB-38, the two pitot tubes were moved to the top of the nose.

The XB-38 is observed from the right rear; no machine guns were mounted in the tail turret. The plane's first flight was on May 19, 1943.

The engine nacelles and propeller spinners of the XB-38 gave the aircraft a sleek and streamlined look. Many Flying Fortress aficionados consider the XB-38 the most beautiful member of the family.

The Allison V-1710-89 engines of the XB-38 were rated at 1,425 horsepower at 25,000 feet and a maximum speed of 327 miles per hour at that altitude, compared with the Wright R-1820-65 Cyclone engines of the B-17E, which produced 1,000 horsepower and a top speed of 318 miles per hour at 25,000 feet.

With the cowling panels removed, engines number 1 and 2 of the XB-38 are exposed to view, showing the ducting for the exhausts and the oil coolers.

The air outlet doors below the Allison engines are open in this photo of engines 3 and 4 on the XB-38.
Also visible are the firewalls.

A new Allison V-1710-89 V-12 engine is seen from the right side, installed on its mount. A strip of material, possibly plywood, is bolted over the exhaust flanges to keep out foreign objects. Below that strip are the spark plugs, spark-plug cooling manifold, and ignition harness. On the front of the engine block are the front and rear gear-reduction cases.

An Allison V-1710-80 engine for an XB-38 is installed on its mount, which in turn is attached to the firewall of an engine nacelle assembly. Built into the bottom of the engine mount was a rather substantial pan of riveted construction that extended under most of the engine.

The XB-38 is seen from the right side during a test flight over mountainous desert terrain, probably in Southern California, in 1943. The nine test flights the XB-38 was subjected to indicated that it had a service ceiling of 29,700 feet, compared to 36,600 feet for the B-17E. However, the XB-38 would have had a better range: 2,400 miles, compared to 2,000 miles for the B-17E.

This in-flight photo of the XB-38 is one of the rare ones that show the turbosuperchargers on the lower rears of the engine nacelles. As may be seen on the outboard side of the nacelle for engine number 3 (*the second from right*), it was still necessary, as with the B-17Es, to route part of the exhausts on the outside of the inboard nacelles because of the limited space in the main landing-gear bays. Also visible is the dummy ball turret installed on the XB-38.

The XB-38 is viewed from above in a photo taken on April 10, 1943. Note the streamlined fairing to the front of the exhaust line on the side of the inboard engine nacelle.

Initial tests of the XB-38 were promising but were terminated when the aircraft crashed and was destroyed near Tipton, California, during its ninth test flight, on June 16, 1943. The crew bailed out, five of the six surviving.

CHAPTER 3
B-17F

The next advance in the B-17 design was the B-17F. But for the frameless, molded Plexiglas nose, the early B-17F appeared essentially identical to the B-17E. However, there were numerous internal improvements introduced with the new model—over 700, in fact. One of the most significant was the utilization of a new model of the Wright Cyclone engine, the R-1820-97, which with the throttle pushed to the War Emergency setting generated 1,380 horsepower. To harness the increased power more efficiently at altitude, new paddle-blade Hamilton Standard propellers were installed. The new propellers, which not only were broader but also 1 inch larger in diameter, required a slight redesign of the cowlings.

The bomber's range was increased to a maximum of 4,220 miles. This was done by allowing for additional fuel tanks, described in the B-17 Pilot Training Manual as such: "There are three tanks in each wing, with provisions for two additional groups of outer wing feeder tanks. These outer wing feeder tanks (Tokyo tanks) are composed of nine individual, collapsible self-sealing cells per wing." The manual goes on to add that "The fuel supply can also be increased by auxiliary installations of releasable fuel tanks in the bomb bay."

Beyond the changes to the airframe itself, there were also numerous changes in the manufacturing process. The most obvious change was the addition of two new manufacturers—Vega and Douglas. The licensed production of the Flying Fortress by these two firms had actually been planned for the B-17E, but that model was superseded by the B-17F before production could actually get underway. Boeing was contracted for 3,735 aircraft on W535-AC-20292, Vega was awarded contract W535-AC-20290, and the Douglas contract was W535-AC-20291. The other major change to the production process was the addition of block numbers. On B-17E aircraft and earlier, the aircraft were simply the given designation; B-17E, for example. However, as various changes were introduced through the course of production, it became too difficult to distinguish the minor variants. The block numbers addressed this by further dividing production by manufacturer and into small groups, or blocks. Thus, the first group of fifty of the new aircraft produced by Boeing was designated B-17F-1-BO, the second group of fifty was B-17F-5-BO, and so forth.

The final B-17E rolled off the Boeing production line on May 28, 1942. Two days later the first B-17F took to the air. Vega was actually able to begin B-17F production before Boeing, and the first Burbank-produced B-17F, B-17F-1-VE, serial number 42-5705, flew on May 4, 1942. Douglas built Flying Fortresses at Long Beach, with their first, B-17F-1-DL, delivered to Wright Field for testing on July 1, 1942.

One of the early criticisms of the B-17, especially from the British, was that for such a large aircraft with a long range, it had only a modest bombload. In an effort to remedy this, provisions for external bomb racks began to be installed at production blocks B-17F-30-BO, B-17F-20-DL, and B-17F-20-VE. These racks were installed beneath the wings, between the fuselage and inboard engines. The aircraft manual shows that each of the two wing racks could support a single 1,000-, 1,600-, 2,000-, or 4,000-pound bomb. The internal bomb bay could carry up to forty-two bombs in sizes from 100 to 2,000 pounds, in varying combinations. The rated maximum short-range bombload was 17,600 pounds, but dimensionally, eight 1,600-pound bombs could be carried internally, along with a pair of 4,000-pound externally carried bombs, giving a theoretical total load of 20,800 pounds. The maneuverability, as well as the range, of the aircraft was considerably hampered by the use of the external bomb racks, so they were used only rarely.

In order to support the increased weight of the aircraft, the landing gear of the B-17F was strengthened first to 65,000-pound capacity, and later to 72,000 pounds.

An astrocompass bubble was added ahead of the windshield, atop the navigator and bombardier's compartment, beginning with the -15 production blocks at Vega and Douglas and the -45 production block at Boeing.

In hopes of staving off frontal attacks, cheek guns began to be installed on the noses of B-17Fs at modification centers prior to their delivery to combat units. These cheek guns were factory installed beginning with Boeing B-17F-55-BO (serial number 42-29467) and Douglas B-17F-15-DL (serial number 42-3004), and at an unknown point by Lockheed-Vega.

However, the cheek guns by themselves were inadequate, and, taking a lesson from the X/YB-40 program described in the next chapter, a Bendix chin turret began to be installed. Although most often associated with the B-17G, these turrets were actually a fixture on the final eighty-six B-17Fs built by Douglas, beginning with serial number 42-3504. These aircraft were so similar to the later B-17G that the 8th Air Force considered them B-17Gs, despite the stenciling to the center of the fuselage.

Ultimately, 3,405 B-17Fs were produced, with Boeing turning out the most with 2,300, while Douglas built 605, and Vega 500.

The B-17F enjoyed a number of distinguishing characteristics: it was the first model of B-17 to be produced by the "BVD" (Boeing, Vega, and Douglas) manufacturing pool. Most noticeably, the B-17F had a single-piece clear nose with no framing except around the flat bomb-aiming window. Provisions were added for external bomb racks. The landing gear was strengthened, and there were hundreds of other changes. It was the first model of Flying Fortress to include production-lot and manufacturer's symbols in the aircraft's nomenclature; thus the serial number of "Miss Barbara," depicted here, 41-24519, designated a B-17F-20-BO, with the number "20" representing the production lot and "BO" standing for Boeing. *National Archives*

As seen on B-17F-50-BO, serial number 42-4561 (*in the foreground*), the new nose introduced on the B-17F lacked the metal frame of its predecessors. The nose was molded of Plexiglas, with a plate-glass bomb-aiming window at the lower center. Early on, the B-17Fs retained the same type and arrangement of cheek windows as the B-17Es. *Library of Congress*

Another new feature introduced with the B-17F was a change to wider-chord "paddle" blades for the Hamilton Standard Hydromatic propellers. The part number of these propeller blades was G6477A-0. Also in view is the front of the number 3 Wright R-1820 Cyclone engine.

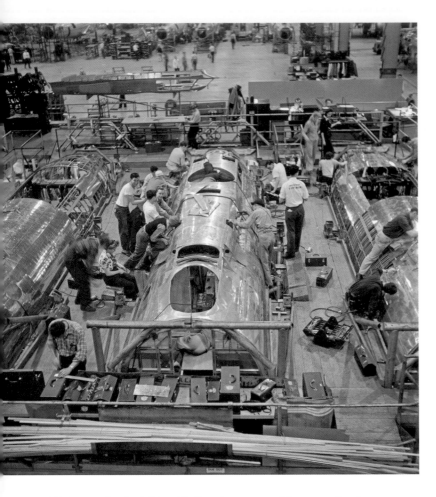

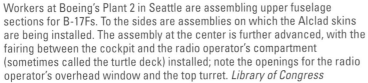

Workers at Boeing's Plant 2 in Seattle are assembling upper fuselage sections for B-17Fs. To the sides are assemblies on which the Alclad skins are being installed. The assembly at the center is further advanced, with the fairing between the cockpit and the radio operator's compartment (sometimes called the turtle deck) installed; note the openings for the radio operator's overhead window and the top turret. *Library of Congress*

A sling is attached to the fuselage section containing the bomb bay of a B-17F (Flying Fortress) bomber preparatory to hoisting it from its cradle and mating it to the section of fuselage containing the radio operator's compartment, at Boeing's Plant 2 in Seattle. In the foreground is bulkhead 4, separating the flight engineer's compartment from the bomb bay. The turtle deck above the radio operator's compartment is being built; note the ribs to each side, each of which has a large lightening hole. *Library of Congress*

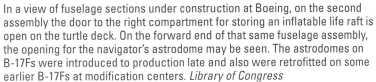

In a view of fuselage sections under construction at Boeing, on the second assembly the door to the right compartment for storing an inflatable life raft is open on the turtle deck. On the forward end of that same fuselage assembly, the opening for the navigator's astrodome may be seen. The astrodomes on B-17Fs were introduced to production late and also were retrofitted on some earlier B-17Fs at modification centers. *Library of Congress*

Details of B-17F fuselage assemblies are visible in this Boeing factory photo, including wing-fuselage joints, cockpits, and bulkheads. In the lower foreground is the fixed upper window of a radio operator's compartment, to the rear of which is a hinged air deflector for diverting the airstream when the radio operator is operating his machine gun. In the background are several B-17Fs with the wings and empennages installed. *Library of Congress*

Fuselage sections for B-17F Flying Fortresses are under assembly at the Boeing Aircraft plant in Seattle in December 1942. *Library of Congress*

As seen in another view of B-17Fs on the Boeing assembly line, the fuselage sections include from the radio compartment forward. *Library of Congress*

Aft fuselage sections for B-17Fs are being prepared for mating with the forward fuselage assemblies at the Boeing plant. The forward parts of the dorsal fins have been installed, and tail turrets will be added later. The three large holes near the rear of each of the fuselage sections are for the torque tubes for the rudder (*top*) and the elevators (*sides*). *Library of Congress*

Another grouping of aft fuselage sections for Boeing B-17Fs is viewed from an elevated position. The right waist window is visible on the side of the second fuselage section from the right. *Library of Congress*

Wright R-1820 Cyclone engines, complete with cowl flaps, are awaiting installation in B-17Fs at Boeing's Plant 2 in Seattle. The B-17Fs up to serial number 41-14503 had the R-1820-64 engines, while subsequent planes had the R-1820-97. *Library of Congress*

Inboard wing sections are being readied for installation on B-17F fuselages at the Boeing plant. Engines have been mounted on the wings in the foreground. The ribs and the spars of the wings were in the form of trusses. *Library of Congress*

A Boeing worker is making an adjustment to a rudder on a B-17F. A clear view is available of the construction of the dorsal fin, the rudder, the rudder trim tab, and the tail turret. Note the ring-and-bead sight aft of the rear window of the turret. *Library of Congress*

Mechanics are working on the cowling structure of the number 3 engine assembly on a Boeing B-17F at the factory. The faces of two workers in the cockpit are visible through the side window. *Library of Congress*

Two Boeing technicians are making connections to the rear of engine number 2 of a B-17F. A Sperry A-1 dorsal turret has been installed to the rear of the cockpit. *Library of Congress*

A B-17F in the latter stage of assembly is viewed from the front at Boeing's factory. A small placard with the number "26" is on each side of the nose. The clear nose of the B-17F had three major sections, made of Plexiglas, which were mated together along visible seams. A Plexiglas stiffener was on each side of the bomb-aiming window. Even the hinged port on the right-hand side of the bomb-aiming window was of all-Plexiglas construction. *Library of Congress*

Mechanics at Boeing are lubricating and servicing the engines of a new B-17F in or before December 1942. Note the three small, round fittings and associated plumbing on the exposed portion of the exhaust line from engine number 2. *Library of Congress*

The engines are being tested on the same B-17F, complete with the same fluid leak on the inboard engine nacelle, at the Boeing factory. From this angle, the nomenclature and data stencil below the aft cheek window may be read: this plane was B-17F-50-BO, serial number 42-5428. This plane would go on to serve with the 342nd Bombardment Squadron, 97th Bombardment Group, based at Biskra, Algeria, and was lost, along with its crew, during a bombing mission over Trapani, Sicily, on April 14, 1943. *Library of Congress*

Boeing mechanics evidently are studying a problem—possibly related to the fluid leak below the exhaust—in the forward part of the left main landing-gear bay of a B-17F that recently has left the assembly line. With the aft panels of the cowling removed, the left side of the engine support is visible at its attachment points to the firewall. *Library of Congress*

Boeing B-17F-50-BO, serial number 42-5428, is seen once again during the same occasion as the preceding two photos, with mechanics working to prepare the plane for delivery to the Army. *Library of Congress*

Douglas Aircraft was one of the three builders of the B-17Fs, and shown here is one of them, B-17F-40-DL, serial number 42-3259, while serving with the 332nd Bombardment Squadron, 94th Bombardment Group, under the nickname "SNAFU" during the period spanning May 10 to July 16, 1943. *Air Force Historical Research Agency*

Boeing B-17F-80-BO, serial number 42-30243, is seen in flight upon completion, judging by the extremely clean appearance of the aircraft. Following delivery to the Army at Cheyenne, Wyoming, on March 5, 1943, the plane served with the 331st Bombardment Squadron, 94th Bombardment Group, and was shot down during a mission over France on July 14, 1943. Note the bomb racks under the inboard wing sections. *Air Force Historical Research Agency*

Boeing-built B-17F-85-BO, serial number 42-30060, was delivered on April 6, 1943. Subsequently, it served successively with several photographic and photographic-mapping groups at Buckley Field, Colorado; McChord Field, Washington; Patterson Field, Ohio; and Grenier Field, New Hampshire. *Air Force Historical Research Agency*

Two B-17Fs from the 322nd Bombardment Squadron, 91st Bombardment Group, are on a mission in 1943. The closer bomber, nicknamed "Mizpah the Bearded Beauty," is B-17F-10-BO, serial number 41-24433 and fuselage code LG-0, while the other plane is "Frisco Jenny," B017F-15-BO, serial number 41-24497. Note the mottling of greenish paint that has been applied at intervals around the wings and on the fuselage and the empennage of each plane; this is more evident on "Mizpah the Bearded Beauty."
National Archives

Artwork of Bugs Bunny with one foot on a bomb adorned the nose of B-17F-27-BO, serial number 42-24619, serving with the 427th Bombardment Squadron, 303rd Bombardment Group. At various times this plane bore the nickname "What's Up Doc" and "Jerry Jinx." The plane and its crew were lost during a bombing mission against German U-boat pens at Lorient, France, on January 23, 1943.
National Archives

The Flying Fortress was able to survive an amazing amount of damage, and "All American," B-17F-5-BO, serial number 41-24406, from the 414th Bombardment Squadron, 97th Bombardment Group, could have been a poster girl for the plane's ruggedness. The huge tear in the empennage and aft fuselage was caused when a Messerschmitt Bf 109 slammed into the bomber during a mission over Tunisia on February 1, 1943.

The midair collision between the Bf 109 and "All American" resulted in the destruction of the bomber's left horizontal stabilizer and elevator. Nonetheless, pilot Lt. Kendrick R. Bragg succeeded in flying the Flying Fortress to the base at Biskra, Algeria.

Boeing B-24F-50-BO, serial number 42-5424 and plane number 177, is undergoing maintenance. Two men are holding the left main wheel while others are working on the left wheel mount. The center cheek window is the enlarged version introduced during B-17F production; it included a mount for a .50-caliber machine gun. On the right side of the nose, a machine gun is mounted in the enlarged forward cheek window, as seen through the clear nose. *National Archives*

A direct hit from enemy flak tore open the fuselage on the left side of the Sperry A-1 dorsal turret. The photo is dated July 28, 1943. Inside the peeled-back aluminum skin next to the turret dome is the support for the turret, with oblong lightening holes in it.

By far the most famous B-17 Flying Fortress, and possibly tied with "Enola Gay" as the most renowned aircraft of World War II, the "Memphis Belle" embodied the can-do spirit of the Army Air Forces men who braved the flak-and-fighter-infested skies of the European theater. The Army Air Forces selected "Memphis Belle," a Boeing B-17F-10-BO, serial number 41-24485, for a publicity campaign to highlight the heavy bombers' and crews' contributions to the war effort, in part because it was one of the first B-17s to complete twenty-five combat missions. The plane and crew returned to the United States for a publicity tour, and famed Hollywood director William Wyler directed a documentary film on the plane. "Memphis Belle" is shown here during a tour stop at National Airport in Washington, DC, in mid-June 1943. *National Archives*

The nose of "Memphis Belle" is shown close-up in a photograph taken on June 16, 1943, at National Airport, Washington, DC. The iconic pinup nose art of the Belle is present. The multitude of details in the photo include the tubular braces for the nose machine guns, the single swastika kill marking below the center cheek window, and the twenty-five bomb markings symbolizing combat missions and eight swastikas representing aircraft kills. Crewmen's names and those of squadron members were painted or scrawled here and there on the plane; even little Stuka, the "Memphis Belle's" Scottish terrier mascot, had his name emblazoned on the forward entry door. *National Archives*

SSgt. Casimer A. Nastal, the right waist gunner of "Memphis Belle," poses for his photograph in his "office" along with the plane's mascot, the Scottish terrier named Stuka, who has found a convenient perch on the receiver of a .50-caliber machine gun. *National Archives*

The left waist gunner of "Memphis Belle," SSgt. Clarence E. "Bill" Winchell, poses at his station during the tour stop of the aircraft and crew at National Airport, Washington, DC, on June 16, 1943. *National Archives*

SSgts. Casimer Nastal, *foreground*, and Clarence Winchell demonstrate the waist gunners' battle stations in "Memphis Belle." The waist windows were directly across from each other, making for very cramped quarters, especially when the gunners were trying to fire at enemy aircraft attacking from both sides at once. *National Archives*

During twenty-four of its combat missions, the ball turret of "Memphis Belle" was manned by SSgt. Cecil H. Scott. On the bottom of the national insignia at the top of the photo are inscribed the names of Maj. William Wyler, director of the *Memphis Belle* documentary for the 1st Motion Picture Unit of the US Army Air Forces, and Capt. William H. Clothier, Wyler's cinematographer, who shot footage in the plane during numerous combat missions and went on to become one of Hollywood's most celebrated cinematographers. *National Archives*

With his crew standing at attention, Capt. Robert K. Morgan, aircraft commander of the "Memphis Belle," shakes hands with Lt. Gen. Jacob L. Devers while Maj. Gen. Ira C. Eaker, *right*, stands by, at RAF Bovingdon, England, on June 9, 1943. The USAAF brass were congratulating the crew before they departed for the United States after completing their twenty-fifth operational flight. *National Archives*

John P. "J. P." Quinlan poses at his station in the tail turret of "Memphis Belle" at National Airport, Washington, DC, on June 16, 1943. The tight headroom of the turret is evident. To Quinlan's front, as he faced to the rear, were two small windows, the lower of which was of bullet-resistant glass. On the rear face of the turret, below the opening for the twin .50-caliber machine guns, are bomb-signal lights. Photos of the "Memphis Belle" during this period show that much of the fuselage surface was spattered with oil. *National Archives*

During the farewell ceremony for the crew of the "Memphis Belle" at RAF Bovingdon, King George VI, partially hidden by his wife, Queen Elizabeth, *center*, is shaking hands with members of the crew of the bomber. *National Archives*

After being displayed outdoors in Memphis, Tennessee, for several decades, the "Memphis Belle" was transferred to the National Museum of the United States Air Force, at Wright-Patterson Air Force Base, Ohio, in 2005. Restoration work was begun at the museum, and "Memphis Belle" was placed on permanent display in the museum's World War II Gallery in May 2018. The venerable bomber is shown on a tarmac at Wright-Patterson.

"Memphis Belle" is viewed from the right following restoration. The tail number, 124485, is a slightly shortened version of its serial number, 41-24485. The paint replicates the splotchy green camouflage over the main Olive Drab color, seen on photos of "Memphis Belle" during World War II.

The scoreboard of missions replicates the final version, with twenty-five yellow bomb symbols representing operational missions. Reportedly the stars above certain bombs represented the "Memphis Belle'" position in the bomber formation for that mission. The swastika below the center cheek window indicates a claimed kill of a German aircraft.

"Memphis Belle" is decorated with a patriotic banner over the nose, and a tractor to the rear of the aircraft is prepared to tow it. The occasion was the move of the aircraft from the hangar where it was restored to the World War II Gallery, on March 18, 2018. The hubcaps with red stars and white cloverleaf pattern over a base color of blue are not present in this photo.

Since 2018, "Memphis Belle" has been on display in the World War II Gallery of the Museum of the United States Air Force. The Flying Fortress is supported on three stands, with landing gear raised. Below the inboard right engine nacelle is a Norden bombsight on display.

The right inboard nacelle is in view, showing how the exhaust was routed on the outside of the nacelle to provide adequate space for the landing gear inside the nacelle. Authentic decals were applied to the aircraft during restoration. *Author*

The ball turret in the restored "Memphis Belle" is viewed from the right side of the fuselage; the turret is trained aft. The dome-shaped side fairings for the turret, with clear panels and metal frame and spokes, which often are missing from restored bombers, are present. *Author*

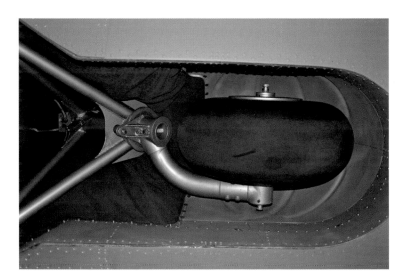

The tail landing gear is seen in its bay. The rear half of the bay is enclosed by a metal fairing, while a canvas boot covering the front part of the bay serves to prevent drafts from streaming into the fuselage. *Author*

The bomb bay of "Memphis Belle" is viewed from below, with a bomb rack on each side, two bomb racks in a V formation at the center, the door into the flight engineer / top gunner's compartment at the upper center, the bomb-bay truss to the left of center, and the forward bomb-bay actuating mechanisms toward the lower corners.

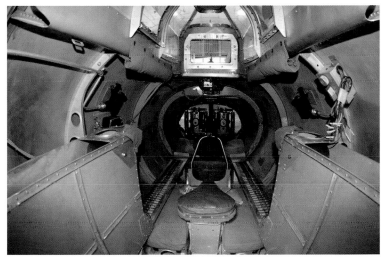

A Browning M2 .50-caliber machine gun is mounted in the left waist window of the "Memphis Belle." Armor plates are bolted to the aircraft frame below the window. To the rear is the .50-caliber ammunition box. In real practice, a flex chute fed ammunition from the box to the gun. To the upper right is the sliding cover for the window, of metal construction with a window in the center.

The tail gunner occupied this very cramped station in the tail, seated on a cushioned, bicycle-type seat (*lower center*) with lower legs resting on pads to the sides of the seat. Ammunition was conducted from the boxes in the foreground, along chutes to the two .50-caliber machine guns (*center background*). Toward the top are Olive Drab-colored crash pads, the gunner's clear enclosure, and, through the rear window, the ring-and-bead sight.

The interior of a dismounted Sperry ball turret is viewed through the open hatch. The two .50-caliber machine guns are not installed; mounting brackets for them are on the sides of the interior. At the top are two hand controls, to the left of which is the crank for the manual elevation gear. At the bottom is the flat window through which the gunner acquired and tracked targets with the gunsight (not installed).

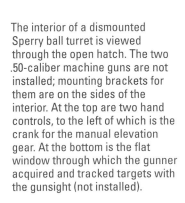

Of about thirty-nine surviving B-17s in the United States, only about a dozen are airworthy, and only one is a B-17F. That example is B-17F-70-BO, serial number 42-29782, now known as "Boeing Bee." Following a three-month tour in England, where it failed to see combat, the plane returned to the United States, finishing the war at Drew Field, Florida. After the war, the plane served as a war memorial in Stuttgart, Arkansas, and a crop duster and firefighter. Currently, the "Boeing Bee" is in the care of the Seattle Museum of Flight. *Tracy White*

Details of the forward-right part of the "Boeing Bee" are in view, including the clear nose with bombsight inside (the red object on the sight is an inverted plastic cup), the enlarged forward cheek window with .50-caliber machine-gun mount, right pitot tube, navigator's astrodome, and cockpit canopy. *Author*

An unpainted LP-21-A radio direction-finder nonstatic loop antenna, commonly called a RDF football antenna because of its shape, is mounted to the left of center under the nose of "Boeing Bee." *Author*

The right pitot tube on the side of the nose of "Boeing Bee" is viewed close-up. A protective cover has been placed over the pitot tube, which, with its mast, forms an L-shaped unit. *Author*

Below the leading edge of the right wing between the fuselage (*right*) and the inboard engine nacelle (*left*) are an air inlet for the right-inboard oil cooler and the ram-air inlet for the supercharger for engine number 3. *Author*

A close-up view of engine number 3 (right inboard) includes details of the cylinders, push rods, ignition harness, and gear-reduction housing, as well as of the Hamilton Standard Hydromatic R-6477A-0 paddle blades, propeller hub, and dome. *Author*

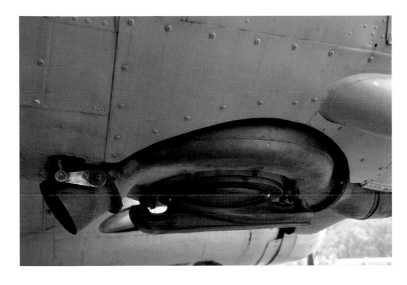

One of the four turbosuperchargers of "Boeing Bee" is depicted in its cutout in the bottom of an engine nacelle. To the left is the waste gate, where engine exhaust is expelled. On the side of the waste gate is a link and lever for operating a butterfly valve inside the gate. *Author*

The left main landing gear is seen from the inboard side. To the left is the oleo strut, which features a shock absorber. To the lower rear of the oleo strut is the antitorque link, which maintains the alignment of the wheel with the fore-aft centerline of the aircraft. *Author*

The right wing is viewed from the rear, showing four slots on the wing top for expelling intercooler air. *Author*

The main landing gears of the B-17F were equipped with Hayes wheels with 20-by-2¾-inch duplex expander tube brakes and 55-by-19-inch tires. The brake line was routed from the hollow axle to the brake. *Author*

The entry door on the right side of the aft fuselage has a window and a stamped inner surface for reinforcing. This door had releasable hinge pins for rapid exit during flight. *Author*

A portable auxiliary generator was carried in the aft part of the fuselage of the B-17F opposite the entry door. It comprised a 28-volt, 70-ampere, 2,000-watt generator driven by a one-cylinder, hand-started gasoline engine. The unit was intended to be operated outside the plane only and was used to provide external power to the aircraft when needed. *Author*

Provisions for storing and directing .50-caliber ammunition to the waist machine guns varied from model to model in the B-17s and sometimes varied within a particular model. Often, the ammo boxes were fabricated from wood and plywood, with metal feed chutes, as seen in this interior view to the rear of the right waist window. *Author*

A typical .50-caliber machine gun mount in the waist positions of a B-17F resembled this unit, with the receiver of the machine gun secured to a cradle referred to as an adapter. The adapter was mounted on a pintle, inserted in the top of a tubular stanchion. A ring-and-bead sight was provided. Handgrips and triggers were to the rear of the receiver, while the charging handle was on the side of the receiver. *Author*

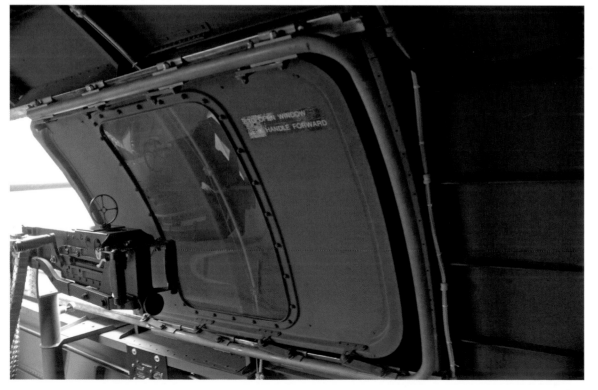

The waist windows of the B-17F were mounted on frames, on which they slid into the interior of the fuselage when opened. The method of fastening the Plexiglas clear panel to the window structure is apparent. *Author*

The Sperry ball turret of the "Boeing Bee" B-17F is viewed from the interior of the aft fuselage, looking down at the spherical enclosure and facing aft. The turret was supported by a structure called the hanger, which was attached to the fuselage frame at the top of the compartment. A yellow oxygen bottle is attached to the hanger. The ball-turret gunner sat in this compartment during takeoffs and landings, entering the turret only when it was in the air. *Author*

The Sperry ball turret of "Boeing Bee" almost touches the ground in this view of the unit traversed to the left. The gunner was provided with a flat, round panel of glass for sighting through. Inside the turret, a steel plate that supported the gunner's seat also served as armor protection for him. *Author*

The layout of instruments and controls in the "Boeing Bee" bears a strong, but perhaps not perfect, resemblance to the original, World War II appearance. *Author*

The navigator's and bombardier's compartment in the nose of "Boeing Bee" is viewed from a low perspective in the rear of the compartment, with the navigator's seat and desk in the foreground and the bombardier's seat and Norden bombsight in the background. In the left background is the bombardier's instrument panel. To the right is a .50-caliber machine gun mounted in the right front cheek window; note the support and the cross brace for the socket mount for this gun. *Author*

CHAPTER 4

X/YB-40

During the early part of the USAAF's involvement in the air war over Europe, the lack of long-range fighter escorts was a serious handicap. Thus, experiments were made with a heavily armed aircraft based on B-17F-1-BO, serial number 41-34341, to assess the practicability of such an aircraft as an escort for long-range, high-altitude bomber formations. The conversion was designated XB-40, and to the basic B-17F it added a remote-controlled chin turret with twin .50-caliber machine guns; a second dorsal-powered turret, above the radio compartment, also with two .50-caliber machine guns; and twin .50-caliber machine guns in the waist windows.

As B-17s began to be used for daylight raids deep into Nazi territory in 1942, a problem quickly arose in that the bombers could outrange the escorting fighters. It did not take long for the enemy to realize this, and soon the bomber crews found that they had uneventful flights up to the point that their escorting fighters had to turn back, at which time they were swarmed by Luftwaffe Messerschmitt Bf 109 and Focke-Wulf Fw 190 fighters. By shear number and calculated tactics, the Germans were able to overwhelm the carefully planned box formations of Flying Fortresses, which were calculated to provide mutual defense for the bombers.

What the 8th Air Force, the primary operator of the B-17 in Europe, needed was an escort with sufficient range to stay with the bombers all the way to the target and back home. Since at that time neither the P-51 Mustang, P-38 Lightning, nor P-47 Thunderbolt had sufficient range, as a possible solution the Army Air Force turned to the B-17 itself. Boeing B-17F, serial number 41-24341, was modified to XB-40 configuration by Vega in November 1942. The modification included mounting two .50-caliber machine guns in each waist position, adding a Bendix chin turret beneath the nose, and adding of a second dorsal turret in the radio compartment. This brought the weapon load up to fourteen .50-caliber heavy machine guns. To feed these weapons, 11,135 rounds of ammunition were carried, although for short-range missions this could be upped to 17,265 rounds. Knowing that the gunship was likely to become a prime target for enemy fighters, additional armor plate was added as well. The modified aircraft first flew on November 10, 1942.

With initially successful tests, twenty-four more aircraft were ordered modified. Four of these were to serve as trainers, while twenty were to be operational test aircraft and thus were designated YB-40. The actual modifications were carried out by Douglas at the modification center in Tulsa, Oklahoma.

Twelve of the YB-40s were sent to England for operational testing. The aircraft were assigned to the 327th Bomb Squadron, the 92nd Bomb Group, the 91st Bomb Group, and the 303rd Bomb Group. The first operational mission was flown on May 29, 1943, with the last on July 29, 1943.

Although, ultimately, gunners aboard YB-40s were credited with kills of five German fighters, as well as two "probables," the program was not considered a success. Heavily laden with guns and ammunition, and suffering from increased drag owing to the additional turrets and gun barrels in the airstream, the YB-40 had a rate of climb half that of a B-17F. Further, while the standard bombers, once unencumbered after releasing their bombs, would scamper home, the YB-40 still was laden with extra armor, turrets, guns, and ammunition. The formations that were to be escorted had to slow down in order for the YB-40 to keep up, increasing the amount of time the formations were over enemy territory.

Accordingly, the YB-40s were withdrawn from service, except for 42-5735, which was lost on a June 23, 1943, raid on the I.G. Farbenindustrie Chemische Werke synthetic rubber plant at Hüls, Germany. Most of the YB-40s that had been sent to Europe were returned to the US and subsequently salvaged at Ontario, California, while the YB-40s and TB-40s that had not gone overseas were scrapped at Walnut Ridge, Arkansas.

The chin turret for the XB-40 was developed by Bendix and was controlled remotely by a gunner seated above the turret. The shape of the turret enclosure was different from the Bendix chin turret later used in the B-17G. Here, the .50-caliber machine gun barrels, which always were subject to corrosion, have a protective wrapping.

The Bendix chin turret of the XB-40 is viewed from the right side. There were continuous slots in the turret shell for both the barrels and for clearance for the gun receivers when the machine guns were elevated. Inside the nose is the chin gunner's station and sight.

On both sides of the fuselage of the XB-40, above the trailing edge of the wing, was Mickey Mouse artwork, with the Disney character waving pistols and festooned with ammo belts, intoning, "LET THEM COME GANG I'LL TAKE CARE OF THEM!" This photo shows the XB-40 with the original configuration of the aft dorsal turret nestled into the rear of the turtle deck.

This XB-40, serial number 41-24341, as viewed from the left side while parked on a snowy airfield, retained the stock Bendix A-1 dorsal turret, the ball turret, and the tail turret of the B-17F.
National Archives

Originally, the second, aft dorsal turret of the XB-40 was nestled into the rear of the turtle deck fairing that extended atop the fuselage from the cockpit to what originally was the radio operator's compartment, but by the time this photo was taken, that fairing had been truncated, and this provided the aft dorsal turret with a better field of fire to the upper front. *National Archives*

The artwork of a gun-slinging Mickey Mouse is shown on the left side of the XB-40's fuselage. A close inspection of the photo at the upper left reveals that the plane is as it was after the turtle deck was shortened. *National Archives*

Twenty service-test YB-40s were produced, converted from airframes of B-17F-10-VE serial numbers 42-5732 to 42-5744; B-17F-30-VE, 42-5871; and B-17F-35-VE, 42-5920, 42-5921, 42-5923, 42-5924, 42-5925, and 42-5927. Shown here is 42-5927, which was painted with aircraft number "253." Note the different shape of the Bendix chin turret on this plane. Also, four TB-40 trainers were converted by Douglas Aircraft at its Tulsa Modification Center. *National Archives*

An airman leads English children in a game of ring-around-the-rosy at a "kiddies' party" next to a YB-40 assigned to the 524th Bombardment Squadron, 379th Bombardment Group, at RAF Kimbolton on October 2, 1943. A companion view of the same plane taken on the same occasion reveals that the tail number was 25736, which equates to the fifth YB-40, converted from B-17F-10-VE, serial number 42-5736. This plane was nicknamed "Tampa Tornado."

CHAPTER 5
B-17G

The final production variant of the Flying Fortress, the B-17G, took to the air over Seattle for the first time on May 21, 1943. However, the first delivery of the model to the Army Air Force was not until September 4, and that aircraft was built by Douglas.

The most readily identifiable characteristic of the model was the Bendix chin turret, which as discussed had previously been used on the X and YB-40 gunships and the final eighty-six B-17Fs built by Douglas. In total, there were 634 engineering changes differentiating the B-17G from the B-17F. Production of the B-17G was undertaken by the triad of Boeing, Vega, and Douglas, with a total of 8,703 of the type being produced, making it by far the most common version of the Flying Fortress.

Like the previous models, the B-17G continued to be improved during its production run. The cheek gun positions became bulged, allowing better sighting. A taller Plexiglas dome with less framework was used on the Sperry A-1 upper turret, and a new tail gun installation was engineered.

Developed at the United Airlines Modification Center in Cheyenne, Wyoming, the new gun provided notably better visibility for the gunner as well as a wider field of fire for the twin .50-caliber machine guns, in addition to adding a reflector sight. Beginning with B-17G-80-BO (43-28473), B-17G-55-VE (44-8287), and B-17G-25-DL (42-37989), the new tail gun installation began to be factory installed, while earlier aircraft were retrofitted at modification centers. Installation of the new mounting reduced the length of the B-17 by 5 inches. Due to the site of its development, the new gun installation has become known as the Cheyenne turret.

Equally important, if not more so, were sweeping changes to the waist gun positions. A sealed waist gun installation was developed, with the gun swiveling on a mounting at the bottom of a large Plexiglas window, thereby eliminating the blast of frigid air that had previously howled through the airplane at altitude. Further, the waist gun positions on late B-17Gs were staggered rather than being back to back, increasing mobility of the gunners, who no longer had to worry about colliding with each other.

The radio compartment gun, always of limited utility owing to its upward, rearward aim with limited visibility and field of fire, was eliminated in the B-17G-105 and -110-BO, B-17G-75 to -85-DL, and B-17G-85 to -110-VE production blocks.

As the air war in Europe wore on, production of the B-17 and competitive B-24 continued to climb. The B-24 offered the advantage of greater bombload, longer range, and combined efforts of five manufacturers, which resulted in it being the most produced bomber ever. However, for air crews in Europe, this was more than a numbers game. A 1944 study by the Army Air Force Operations and Requirements Division concluded "it would be desirable to increase B-17 production and decrease that of the B-24, because the former airplane is a much more effective combat weapon."

A 1944 study by the AAF Unit Training Division was summarized by Col. R. R. Walker, chief of the Unit Training Division, with this harsh criticism: "The extensive use of the B-24 is inconsistent with the blunt fact that it is the most extravagant killer of any airplane in the AAF." He further stated: "Had the B-24 had as good accident rate as the B-17 during the period December 7, 1941, through September 1944, there would have been a saving of 230 aircraft wrecked, 904 lives, and approximately $60,000,000."

Maj. Gen. James Doolittle, commander of the 8th Air Force and, given his leading the historic raid on Tokyo in 1942, certainly no stranger to risk, wrote to Lt. Gen. Carl Spaatz, commander US Strategic Forces in Europe, concerning the B-24. In his letter of February 14, 1944, Doolittle stated that if the type was to be used "conventionally in this theater, immediate remedial action must be taken through extensive local modifications and substantial changes in design must be accomplished now even though this may necessitate a reduction in production."

In view of the coming invasion of Europe and the all-out effort being made to muster airpower, Spaatz, with the support of Gen. H. H. Arnold, rejected Doolittle's request. Ultimately, however, Doolittle was able to begin the replacement of the B-24 in the European theater of operations (ETO) with more B-17s, with the B-17G being instrumental in this change. By VE-Day, there were 2,300 B-17Gs in England.

Boeing delivered their last B-17G on April 13, 1945, concentrating their efforts on the new B-29 Superfortress. Outstanding orders for 130 B-17s were canceled with Vega, as were orders for 600 that had been placed with Douglas.

Following World War II, the B-17 was rapidly removed from service as a strategic bomber, replaced by the new B-29. Most of those that were retained served as drones or reconnaissance aircraft, flying with various designations of QB-17, F-9C, or RB-17G.

The B-17G was the final model of the Flying Fortress as well as the most numerous, with Boeing, Douglas, and Vega completing a total of 8,703 planes. The main distinguishing characteristic was the Bendix-powered chin turret, operated by the bombardier. After early production, the Sperry A-1 dorsal turret received a taller clear dome. Only one pitot tube was present, on the left side of the nose. Depicted here is B-17G-5-BO, serial number 42-31207, with the original, low dorsal turret dome.

As seen in a photo of an early B-17G taken on June 15, 1944, early G-model planes were not equipped with cheek machine guns, since the Army thought that the chin turret would cover the same fields of fire as the cheek guns. However, during production, new cheek machine-gun mounts and windows were introduced, with many of these units being retrofitted at modification centers and in the field.

Norden Bombsight M-1

In the B-17G, the bombardier sat on a swiveling seat, the legs of which were attached to a structure called the "spider," which, with the drum-shaped structure it was fastened to, formed the turret support structure. Plexiglas windows and the amplidyne-controlled turret-traversing motor were on the top of the drum; a hydraulic swivel-gland assembly was mounted at the center of the spider to provide uninterrupted flow of hydraulic fluid into the turret as it was traversed. To the front of the seat is a Norden bombsight under cover. To the upper right of the photo is the bombardier's turret controller. The gunsight for the chin turret is out of view in the upper part of the clear nose.

The Norden bombsight—the M1 model is shown here—was one of the United States' prized secret weapons of World War II, part of a system that also included an autopilot and a computer, which permitted extremely accurate bomb aiming. As seen here from the rear, the upper part is the sight head, with the eyepiece at the top center. The sight head pivoted on the lower element, the stabilizer, which contained a directional gyro.

Vega-built B-17G-1-VE, serial number 42-39843, exhibits the red-bordered US insignia briefly used in mid-1943, as well as the original types of windows in the bombardier's and navigator's compartment without machine gun mounts. The early type of dorsal turret dome also is present.

"Dreambaby," as B-17G-35-BO, serial number 42-32025 and fuselage code VP-P, *foreground*, was nicknamed, and a B-17G coded VP-W fly above the English countryside. The VP code pertained to the 533rd Bombardment Squadron, while the black triangle with the white "L" on the tail signified the 381st Bombardment Group. The dark-colored frame of the front cheek window is characteristic of retrofitted window / gun mount units. The late-type waist window is also a retrofit, and the original turret has been replaced by the so-called Cheyenne tail turret, installed both at Eastern Airlines Modification Center in Cheyenne, Wyoming, and at modification centers in England. *National Archives*

The left side of the forward fuselage of "Queenie," B-17G, serial number 42-3135 and fuselage code LG-Q, from the 322nd Bombardment Squadron, 91st Bombardment Group, was photographed in the winter of 1943 at RAF Bassingbourn, England. Three small bombs signifying combat missions are painted to the rear of the cheek machine-gun window. *Roger Freeman*

"Goin Jessies" was a very early B-17G-1-BO, serial number 42-31051, seen here with its crew from the 100th Bombardment Group on February 2, 1944. It was with a different crew that the plane crashed at Elsten, Germany, on June 3, 1944, with seven of the crewmen being killed and three becoming POWs. *US Air Force Academy*

"Latest Rumor" was the nickname of B-17G-40-BO, serial number 42-97126, assigned to the 351st Bombardment Squadron, 100th Bombardment Group. It carried pinup art of a girl on a telephone, as well as a shark's mouth on the chin turret and lower nose.
US Air Force Academy

Boeing B-17G-1-BO, serial number 42-31066, nicknamed "Fools Rush In," forms the backdrop for a group portrait of its crew on January 30, 1944. The plane, which served with the 351st Bombardment Squadron, 100th Bombardment Group, was lost with a different crew aboard after being hit by flak and colliding with a B-17G, serial number 43-38124, during a mission to Hamburg, Germany, on December 31, 1944. Three members of the crew of "Fools Rush In" survived.
US Air Force Academy

"Nine O Nine" was the moniker of B-17G-30-BO, serial number 42-31909, from the 323rd Bombardment Squadron, 91st Bomb Group. It completed an impressive 140 combat missions and is thought to hold the record for the plane with the most completed missions in the 8th Air Force. Here, ground crewmen are servicing engines 2 and 3 and the chin turret, and one of them is painting yet another "combat-mission completed" bomb on the forward fuselage. *Air Force Historical Research Agency*

Pathfinders—radar-equipped bombers that led and directed other bombers on bombing runs—were a useful tool for keeping up continuous bombing operations during overcast weather. This B-17G was equipped with an experimental H2X radome on a structure under the forward fuselage, allowing clearance for the chin turret. In actual practice, Pathfinder B-17Gs would have the H2X radome mounted in place of the ball turret. *Air Force Historical Research Agency*

Vega-built B-17G-40-VE, serial number 42-97991, flies over a mountain range around the time of its delivery in late April 1944. The waist window has been faired over with solid metal, and the original-type tail turret is present. The taller dome for the dorsal turret, introduced with the B-17G, is evident. This plane would be shot down in action over Germany on August 24, 1944. *Air Force Historical Research Agency*

An unidentified B-17G parked on an airfield tarmac exhibits the original configuration of windows for the bombardier's and navigator's compartment, as well as the tall dome for the dorsal turret. Antiglare panels have been painted on the inner surfaces of the engine nacelles. The RDF "football" antenna was mounted farther aft on the bottom of the forward fuselage than on the B-17F.

Armorers are loading bombs in a B-17G. In the foreground is a Chevrolet M6 bomb-service truck with two M5 bomb trailers hitched in tandem to it, loaded with bombs. On the vertical tail is the white "A" in a black triangle symbol of the 91st Bombardment Group. *National Archives*

Boeing B-17G-70-BO, serial number 43-37716, was the 5,000th B-17 to be manufactured by that corporation after the December 7, 1941, Japanese attack on Pearl Harbor, and as such, the plane was named "5GRAND." The fuselage is shown here on the assembly line, covered with the names of those workers who were involved with the plane's construction.

After completion, "5GRAND" was displayed outdoors at the Boeing factory, complete with temporary signage celebrating the plane's status. The names of workers covered virtually every surface, but the control surfaces, including the rudders, were off limits at this point, although names were later painted on at least the rudder. *Air Force Historical Research Agency*

Hundreds of workers wrote their names in various colors on "5GRAND," in some cases writing over existing names. Also visible on the aluminum skin of the plane are the Alclad stencils, painted numerous times on each panel. *Air Force Historical Research Agency*

Several women mechanics are making final adjustments to "5GRAND" at the Boeing plant, with other B-17Gs lined up in the background. Machine guns were installed, with paper and tape wrappings on the gun barrels. *Air Force Historical Research Agency*

"5GRAND" flies above the clouds before receiving unit markings. Later, it would serve with the 338th Bombardment Squadron, 96th Bombardment Group, in England, where it would complete seventy-eight combat missions. After the war, "5GRAND" and its crew performed a war bond tour of the United States before it was scrapped at Kingman, Arizona. *Air Force Historical Research Agency*

"Yankee Belle," *foreground*, B-17G-35-BO, serial number 42-32085 and fuselage code DF-K, flies in formation with other B-17Gs of the 324th Bombardment Squadron, 91st Bombardment Group, based at Bassingbourn, England. Later transferred to the 322nd Bombardment Squadron, this plane was lost during a combat mission over Germany on February 2, 1945; the nine crewmen became prisoners of war. *Roger Freeman*

Vega B-17G-80-VE, serial number 44-8781, was equipped as a Pathfinder, with an H2X radome on its belly. The tail turret is the Cheyenne type. It is shown here with the "MZ" code of the 413th Bombardment Squadron and the C-in-a-square tail symbol of the 96th Bombardment Group. *Roger Freeman*

Flying in formation with other Flying Fortresses from the 447th Bombardment Group, B-17G-60-VE, serial number 44-8393, a Pathfinder from the 709th Bombardment Group, releases its bombs over a cloud-covered target. The other bombers will release their bombs, taking their cue from the Pathfinder. *Roger Freeman*

During an exhibition celebrating the Allied victory in World War II, a photographer snapped this photo of a B-17G from the 94th Bombardment Group from the Eiffel Tower in Paris. No special efforts were made to spruce up the plane, which exhibits heavy weathering and erosion to the red and yellow paint. *Roger Freeman*

An airman is in the dorsal turret of a B-17G. This photo provides a close view of the late-type clear dome of the Sperry A-1 turret. *Roger Freeman*

A B-17G-55-BO, serial number 42-102598, nicknamed "Super Rabbit," crashed at RAF Thorpe Abbots when the copilot retracted the landing gear by mistake while landing after a raid on Merseburg, Germany, on July 28, 1944. The crash landing wrecked the chin turret, damaged the bottom of the fuselage, and bent the propellers, among other damage. "Super Rabbit" was salvaged two days later. *US Air Force Academy*

Boeing B-17G-55-BO, serial number 42-102547, assigned to the 367th Bombardment Squadron, 306th Bombardment Group, at RAF Thurleigh, England, was named "Rose of York," in honor of Princess Elizabeth, later to become Queen Elizabeth II. On July 6, 1944, Princess Elizabeth visited Thurleigh for the official christening of the plane. She is shown here being introduced to members of the plane's crew.

Princess Elizabeth poses with a USAAF officer during the christening ceremony for "Rose of York" on July 6, 1944. A metal plate has been attached to the chin machine guns for breaking the ceremonial champagne bottle on. Note the Olive Drab cloth covers for the two slots on the chin-turret shell, with zippers on the covers. As the guns elevated and depressed, the zippers moved with them, keeping the covers closed at all times. *Roger Freeman*

The 6,981st and final Flying Fortress built by Boeing in Seattle came in for the VIP treatment, being decorated with commemorative signage and multicolored stickers printed with the names of cities and places the Flying Fortresses had bombed in all theaters of combat during the war. In the background is a Boeing B-29 similarly decorated. *Air Force Historical Research Agency*

A P-51 Mustang escorts a restored B-17G nicknamed "Fuddy Duddy." This is a Douglas-built B-17G-85-DL, serial number 44-83563, that was delivered to the Army on April 7, 1945. The plane served as a staff transport until 1955. It has been repainted to replicate "Fuddy Duddy" B-17G-85-DL, serial number 44-83563. *Rich Kolasa*

Completed in November 1944, "Sentimental Journey" is a surviving B-17G-85-DL, serial number 44-83514, which now flies with the Commemorative Air Force out of Mesa, Arizona. The nose art features a likeness of actress Betty Grable, a favorite pinup of the troops in World War II. It has a Cheyenne tail turret and bears the triangle-U symbol of the 457th Bombardment Group on the tail. *Rich Kolasa*

Vega B-17G-110-VE, serial number 44-85829, is one of the flightworthy G-model Flying Fortresses and operates under the ownership of the Yankee Air Museum with the nickname "Yankee Lady." Delivered in July 1945, the plane did not see service in World War II. In the postwar years, it served with the US Coast Guard as an air-sea rescue aircraft and, later, as a firefighting plane for a private company. It is painted in markings for the 534th Bombardment Squadron, 381st Bombardment Group (Triangle L), 8th Air Force, based at RAF Ridgewell, England, in late 1944, but the "Yankee Lady" name and nose art are generic. *Rich Kolasa*

"Yankee Lady" is viewed close-up in flight. During restoration, the airframe required much rebuilding, including eliminating a large cargo door in the fuselage, installing new fabric on control surfaces, restoring some bulkheads and floors to original configurations, overhauling the engines, and installing cables and other systems to ensure flight safety. Significantly, all turrets had been removed in the postwar years, and replacements were found and installed, including a Cheyenne tail turret. *Rich Kolasa*

"Fuddy Duddy," B-17G-85-L, serial number 44-83563, has nose art of cartoon character Elmer Fudd on each side of the forward fuselage. Two nonoriginal blade antennas are on the turtle deck between the top turret and the dorsal fin. *Rich Kolasa*

"Liberty Belle," Vega B-17G-105-VE, serial number 44-85734, was another G-model Flying Fortress that was delivered too late to see combat in World War II. After the war, Pratt & Whitney used this plane as a flying test bed. Restoration of the airframe began in the 1990s by the Liberty Foundation, and it once again began flying in 2004. It was given replica markings for a historic B-17G nicknamed "Liberty Belle," serial number 42-97849, which was assigned to the 570th Bombardment Squadron, 390th Bombardment Group, in World War II. On June 13, 2011, "Liberty Belle" caught fire after making an emergency landing, causing severe damage to the entire plane. The remains were preserved, with the intention of rebuilding the aircraft. *Rich Kolasa*

Boeing B-17G-35-BO, serial number 42-32076, was accepted on January 19, 1944, and flew its first combat mission on March 24, 1944, with the 91st Bombardment Group from RAF Bassingbourn, England. Originally nicknamed "Shoo Shoo Baby," after a popular song by the Andrews Sisters, the plane was renamed "Shoo Shoo Shoo Baby" in May 1944. On its twenty-fourth combat mission, the plane crash-landed at Malmö Airport, Sweden; the Swedish government interned the plane and crew. Subsequently, the Swedes converted "Shoo Shoo Shoo Baby" to a transport plane before selling her to a Danish company, which later sold it to a French concern. The French donated the plane to the US Air Force in 1974, and it was later restored. When photographed, the plane was on display at the National Museum of the US Air Force at Wright Patterson Air Force Base, Ohio. In the future, the plane is to be placed on permanent display at the Steven F. Udvar-Hazy Center, National Air and Space Museum.

Owned and flown by the Gulf Coast Wing of the Commemorative Air Force in Conroe, Texas, "Texas Raiders" is a very late-production Douglas B-17G-95-DL, serial number 44-83872. After World War II, the plane was converted to a PB-1W patrol bomber. From the late 1950s to the 1960s, it served as an aerial-surveying aircraft for private concerns. The Confederate Air Force (now the Commemorative Air Force) bought the plane in the late 1960s and restored it. *Rich Kolasa*

Douglas B-17G-85-DL, serial number 44-83575, missed out on combat in World War II but served in the 1st Rescue Squadron and the Military Air Transport Service during the Cold War. In 1952, it was fitted with sensors and subjected to nuclear-bomb tests. In the 1960s, it was restored and used as a fire-bomber. Since 1986, the Collings Foundation was owned the plane, flying it as "Nine O Nine," painted to replicate a B-17G-30-BO of the same nickname (serial number 42-31909; previously depicted herein) that served with the 323rd Bombardment Squadron, 91st Bombardment Group. It was restored to its original appearance by Tom Reilly Vintage Aircraft. The plane survived a serious crash in 1987, but was destroyed in a fatal crash in October 2019. *Author*

The Lone Star Flight Museum, Houston, Texas, owns and flies B-17G-105-VE, serial number 44-85718, painted and marked to replicate a historic B-17G-25-DL, serial number 42-38050, nicknamed "Thunderbird," which was assigned to the 359th Bombardment Squadron, 303rd Bombardment Group, and was scrapped after the end of World War II. "Thunderbird" is viewed from the upper right during a flight. *Rich Kolasa*

The nose of "Nine O Nine" is viewed close-up, showing the arrangements of the cheek machine guns, the clear nose, and the chin turret. In view inside the clear nose are the Norden bombsight, the bombardier's seat, the chin-turret control column (*left*), and the bomb-door and bomb-release controls (*right*). *Author*

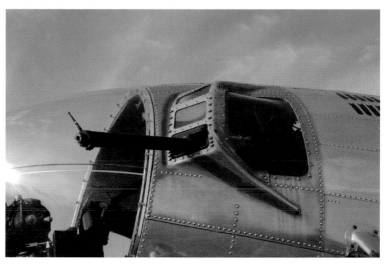

The design of the left cheek machine-gun mount on a B-17G is displayed, with the gun mounted on a reinforced metal protrusion to the front of the main window. Two small, rectangular sighting windows are above the gun. *Author*

The left side of the nose of "Shoo Shoo Shoo Baby" is displayed, complete with a mannequin of a bombardier in flight suit inside. Sometimes blast tubes were mounted on the muzzles of the .50-caliber chin machine guns, as seen here, to protect the clear nose from blast damage. With the chin machine guns elevated, the rears of their receivers are protruding through the slots, made for that purpose, at the rear of the turret shell. Farther aft is the forward-fuselage crew entry door.

The right side of "Fuddy Duddy" is displayed, showing the cheek machine-gun mount and windows, the pitot tube, the chin turret and the fairing to the rear of it, and the clear nose. On the right-hand side of the triangular bomb-aiming window is a small, round door, through which the bombardier could reach out and clean the bomb-aiming window when necessary. *Author*

The right waist machine-gun station in a B-17G is depicted. The sliding window is the early type, with a substantial metal frame with a rectangular window in the center. In the center foreground is a plywood ammunition box. The right waist .50-caliber machine gun is in the travel position. To the far left, part of the ball turret and its support are visible. *Author*

This is a late-model right waist window and machine-gun mount in a B-17G: a large, single-piece, fixed window with a swiveling mount for the machine gun in the lower center. *Author*

Several successive designs of waist windows were employed on B-17Gs. This model was an intermediate one that was fixed in place, with the machine gun on a swivel mount installed directly on the window frame, with windows above and to the sides of the gun mount.

A late-type right waist window is seen, with the right wing visible through the window. The .50-caliber machine gun is in an E-13 adapter (the light-colored, tubular frame), which is installed in a K-6 mount, the base of which is bolted to the window sill. The gun is fitted with a K-13 compensating sight. *Author*

Late-production B-17Gs solved the problem of waist gunners getting in each other's way, by staggering the windows. As seen from aft of the windows, the right one was farther forward than the left one, giving the gunners much more room to maneuver. In the background is the top of the ball turret and its support frame, the top of which is attached to a bracket fastened to the fuselage frame. *Rich Kolasa*

A Sperry ball turret on a restored B-17G is displayed, with the open left door of the bomb bay in the background. The .50-caliber machine gun barrels protrude from the ball. On the side is one of the two trunnion brackets, which provide the mechanical joints for elevating and depressing the turret.

The Sperry ball turret of a B-17G is traversed to the rear, showing the gunner's entry/exit door. Often on later-production B-17s, the clear, curved panels on the sides of the ball turret were left off, exposing the flat sides of the turret. The rear of the bomb bay is at the top of the photo. *Author*

Between the gun barrels of the ball turret is a flat, round sighting window. On the lower part of the ball are ejector ports for spent .50-caliber cartridges and links. *Author*

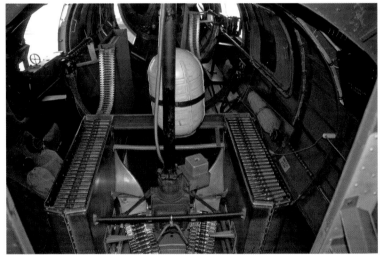

The support structure of the ball turret in a B-17G is viewed facing aft. Early-type Sperry ball turrets carried the ammunition for the twin .50-caliber machine guns inside the turret enclosure; late-type ball turrets had the ammunition boxes mounted above the enclosure, as seen here. *Author*

An early-type tail turret is viewed from aft on a B-17G. To the rear of the small, rectangular sighting window is a ring-and-bead gunsight that moved in unison with the movement of the .50-caliber machine guns. On the Neutral Gray lower rear face of the turret are two bomb-signal lights, used as visual signals to pilots of following bombers when the bomb-bay doors were open (white light) and when the bombs were being released (red). *Author*

An Olive Drab canvas boot is installed over the opening at the rear of an early-type ball turret on a B-17G. The ring-and-bead sight, which was cable-operated, may be seen from another angle; the ring part of the sight is missing. A removable, oblong access panel is to the rear of the sight. *Author*

A mirrorlike finish is on the Cheyenne turret of Vega B-17G-110-VE, serial number 44-85829, now flying as "Yankee Lady." The N-8 reflecting sight is visible inside the rear section of the turret canopy. Details of the empennage also are available. *Rob Ervin*

A Cheyenne tail turret on the B-17G restored to resemble "Liberty Belle" is viewed close-up. The Cheyenne turret had several advantages over the original tail turret, including much-better visibility for the gunner because of the larger windows, better gunner control over the manually operated machine guns because of being mounted closer to the gunner, and a better gunsight: the N-8 reflecting sight. The guns swung up and down in slots in a blister-type housing that traversed from side to side along with the guns. *Rich Kolasa*

The left flap of a B-17G is lowered, revealing details of the interior of the structure. The flaps were articulated so that as they were lowered, the leading edges moved aft. Running along the top (or forward part) of the flap is the torque tube. *Author*

A late-type Sperry turret dome is displayed on a restored B-17G. Also in view are the left side of the cockpit and, aft of the turret, the door to a compartment containing an inflatable life raft. The extensive use of rivets in the construction of the Flying Fortress is evident. *Author*

Early B-17Gs featured the Sperry A-1 dorsal turret with the low Plexiglas dome and complicated frame. An example, specifically of a Sperry A-1A turret, is seen from the front. *Author*

The Sperry A-1A dorsal turret shown in the preceding photo is viewed in its entirety in a display setting, with a clear enclosure around it. Below the upper part of the turret is the lower structure of the turret, which was inside the engineer's compartment aft of the cockpit. On this structure is the gunner's oxygen tank, bags for collecting spent cartridges, and ammunition boxes.

Three AN-M43 500-pound demolition bombs are loaded on a rack in the bomb bay of a restored B-17G. Stencils on the bombs provided nomenclature, lot numbers, and other data. Typical graffiti is visible on the top and bottom bombs. *Author*

The aft-left part of the bomb bay of a B-17G is displayed with the left bay door open. The bay doors were opened and closed using a bomb-door electrical motor that operated a system of shafts, gear boxes, and retracting screws; those for the left door are in view. *Author*

The radio compartment is immediately aft of the bomb bay, with the door into the bomb bay to the right of the photo. On the front left side of the compartment, as seen here, was a seat for the radio operator and a table with a telegraph key mounted on its right side (partially hidden by the open door) and a liaison radio receiver mounted on its front end. On the left fuselage wall are an oxygen regulator and hose and an intercom control box.

A view of a B-17G cockpit provides an overall view of the main instrument panel, with pilot's instruments to the left and copilot's to the right. The hubs of the steering wheels are equipped with B-17 logo plates. Between the control columns is the pedestal, with controls for the throttles, fuel mixture, propellers, lights, and more.

On the left wall of the cockpit, clad with insulating material, is an electrical panel containing four ammeters, light switches, master battery switches, a voltmeter, and various other switches. Aft of that panel are the vacuum pump control and the pilot's oxygen regulator.

The copilot's side of the cockpit is shown, including the seat, the oxygen and intercom controls on the sidewall, and the sliding window on the side of the canopy. Rudder pedals are below the instrument panel.

On the ceiling of the cockpit, between the overhead windows, are, *front to rear*, a panel with a clock, a compass, and a free-temperature gauge; panels with radio-tuning controls and dials; and the command receiver control unit. *Author*

The bombardier's station in the nose of a B-17G is seen from the rear, with the bombardier's seat and the controls for the chin machine gun to the left and the right cheek machine gun, ammunition chute, and ammo box at the center. Toward the right is a portable oxygen cylinder and regulator in a canvas bag. *Author*

In a photo taken next to the navigator's table in the nose of a B-17G, the left cheek .50-caliber machine gun is above the bombardier's instrument panel. The machine gun is mounted in an assembly called an adapter, which included a buffered frame to absorb some of the recoil of the gun. On the rear of the adapter are grips and triggers. *Author*

CHAPTER 6
B-17H/SB-17G

While the B-17G was the final Flying Fortress model to be factory produced, it was not the final B-17 model number, that distinction belonging to the B-17H.

The B-17H was a Flying Fortress especially configured for air-sea rescue work. The concept was first tested in November 1943. As a result of those tests, on June 10, 1944, Higgins Industries of New Orleans was awarded a sole-source contract to produce 600 of the 27-foot, twin-engine, A-1 airborne lifeboat for use on these aircraft. This order was ultimately reduced to 300 of the boats.

These vessels were self-righting and self-bailing and were outfitted with full emergency provisions. Three parachutes were used to drop the boats, which were carried beneath the belly of modified B-17Gs. The boat reached from the rear of the chin turret fairing to the ball turret and was designed to fit snuggly against the underside of the B-17.

To carry the boats, 130 B-17Gs were ordered converted, the modified aircraft to be designated B-17H. In the new role, the chin turret was replaced with a search radar installation.

The B-17H did not become operational until the final months of the war, with the first actual field use of the aircraft taking place off the coast of Denmark in April 1945. The B-17H was also used in the Pacific, where they frequently provided welcome relief to downed B-29 and P-51 crews.

Following VJ-Day, the B-17H variants were among the handful of B-17s kept operational by the US military. In 1948, as part of the reclassification by the new US Air Force, the type was redesignated SB-17G. In many if not all cases, the armament, including upper and ball turrets, was removed during the postwar service. However, when the Korean War again put these aircraft in harm's way, in the early days of the war they served as all-weather reconnaissance aircraft, having the required range. Through spring 1951, they also served their intended purpose, staying aloft along B-29 flight routes from Japan and dropping the venerable A-1 lifeboats to airmen in need.

The B-17H was a conversion of the B-17G for use in air-sea rescue. There is much controversy over how many conversions were completed, with estimates running from twelve to a seemingly more widely accepted total of 130 of these aircraft converted. A feature of the B-17H was the air-droppable A-1 lifeboat, of which Higgins Industries of New Orleans, Louisiana, was the sole contractor. The belly and upper turrets are in place on "Pacific Tramp 2," appropriately operating off Japan. *San Diego Air and Space Museum*

Douglas B-17H-DL, serial number 44-83719, stirs up dust as it taxis at Hayward Airport, California, on April 20, 1947. The "AIR RESCUE SERVICE" stenciling on the A-1 lifeboat is plainly visible, as in the radome of the search radar mounted in the former location of the bomber's chin turret. *Bill Larkins*

An SB-17G with markings for the Air Rescue Service on the upper fuselage is equipped with a radome on the chin and an RDF "football" antenna above the cockpit.

Douglas B-17H-DL, serial number 44-83719, stirs up dust as it taxis at Hayward Airport, California, on April 20, 1947. The "AIR RESCUE SERVICE" stenciling on the A-1 lifeboat is plainly visible, as in the radome of the search radar mounted in the former location of the bomber's chin turret. *Bill Larkins*

SB-17G, serial number 44-85746, has landed on the Rub' al Khali Desert in Saudi Arabia during 1950. Note the slots in the bomb-bay doors to allow the lifeboat-mounting fixtures to protrude. When this photo was taken, this aircraft was serving with Flight D, 7th Air Rescue Squadron, based at Dharan Airfield, Saudi Arabia.

The spectacular scenery of Waikiki Beach and the mountains behind Honolulu form the backdrop of this photo of SB-17G, serial number 44-83773. Marked on the yellow band around the midships part of the fuselage is "AIR RESCUE" over "UNITED STATES AIR FORCE."

Boeing SB-17G, serial number 43-39437, flies abreast of a mountain range in Alaska. The Cheyenne tail turret has been disarmed.

At the same desert site shown in the photo at bottom right on page 125, an SB-17G is taking off. A "USAF" marking is visible under the left wing. On January 19, 1952, three crewmen lost their lives when this SB-17G crashed on the Olympic Peninsula in Washington.

The US Coast Guard also operated the B-17H, designating the type PB-1G. Here, the last Flying Fortress in Coast Guard service poses next to the first HC-130B, its replacement in the air-sea rescue role, at Coast Guard Air Station Elizabeth City in 1959.
US Coast Guard

In World War II the United States managed to marshal its industrial and financial might to produce an amazingly large and increasingly excellent inventory of military equipment, including B-17s by the thousands. The United States also was blessed by a large, talented, and patriotic pool of men and women to manufacture and operate the machinery of war. At the end of the war, much of that equipment was worn out or obsolete, and B-17s by the thousands, including many in this aerial photo of the Army air base at Walnut Ridge, Arkansas, were consigned to long-term storage, sale to civilian concerns, or scrapping.